The Wind
that Shakes the Barley

ELIZABETH MARTINA BISHOP

ISBN-13: 978-1519778383
ISBN-10: 1519778384

BISAC: Poetry / General

Design by Artline Graphics, Sedona AZ, USA
www.artline-graphics.com

The Wind that Shakes the Barley

ELIZABETH MARTINA BISHOP

TABLE OF CONTENTS

PART 1

First Breath,
Last Breath

PART 2
How Eagerly He Recalled Demeter's Passing!

PART 3

Why Doesn't the Body Remember How to Dance?

PART 4

You Haven't a Clue as to How to Play House!

First Breath,

PART
I

Last Breath

First Breath, Last Breath

I know I've lived before, no kidding.
What should I do to bend the antiphons?
What can I accomplish to do your bidding?
Should I lean on one foot like a wise heron?

What should I do to bend the antiphons?
Whatever the case, harvesting the moment,
Leaning on one foot like a wise heron,
Listen to the message you were sent.

Whatever the case, harvesting the moment,
Glancing at your reflection in a pond,
Do you listen to the message you've been lent
And sanctify the blessings of beyond?

Glancing at your reflection in a pond,
In a parallel life you've pawned for gold,
Why subtract the soul-helmet on loan?
Why not settle for a wand of marigold?

In a parallel life you've pawned for gold,
What can I accomplish to do your bidding?
Why not settle for a sprig of marigold?
I know I've lived before, no kidding.

Tennis Rackets and Snow Shoes

I suspect the play offs will reveal the mean
Rehearsing elegiac verses between muse and muse
What shatters a pawn may coerce a reluctant queen

While witnessing a vaguely comedic scene
Even a mermaid's tale lovers may then refute
I suspect the play offs will reverse the mean

Behold the cosseted Vlad the Impaler, calm and serene
Emboldening his sacerdotal dreams, no one can afford to lose
Nor can any chieftain refuse a scantily clad Ondine?

Which infidels agree to flat-line encroaching warrior triremes?
Though winners and losers may endure a similar short-lived fuse
I suspect the play offs will reveal the fated mean

No matter the cost of fragile coffin length unseen
Clay feet stop short of a massacre at the foot of virginal Cross
What shatters the last retort of a bare-chested queen

Who ends up robbing a blind man's sleeping feline
But a seer desperate to strike fear in a recluse
I suspect the play offs will reveal the mean
What matters now and again matters less
Only when jury members are recused and convened.

Night Blindness

Blind-siding Martha, the deer ran across her car.
An oval light once birthed, the deer fled its witness.
Her windshield shattered, Martha recited prayers,
Among the vast unthinking parabolas of kindness.

Where once an oval light had tumbled, darkness stood.
When a soul collapsed an animal torso of prayer,
Disowning vast gardens of parabolas of air,
In twenty seconds, satyr reduced to martyr.

His soul collapsing his body's animal prayer,
In the liquid light of evening, misunderstood,
When in twenty seconds, satyr reduced to martyr,
Fate summons a phantom from a wood.

In the limpid light of evening, misunderstood,
What could be done to steer a battered car?
Fate summons a phantom from a wood.
Long forgotten, the pattern of the dog star.

What could be done to steer a battered car?
The windshield shattered, alerted, Martha recited prayers.
Long-forgotten, the pattern of the dog star.
Blind-siding Martha, a deer once ran across her car.

Plague

The accursed room was filled with critters, I swear!
It doesn't take a course in rocket science,
To know when you're being eaten alive, my dear.
When russet skin's aflame, how tackle self-reliance?

It doesn't take a course in rocket science,
My friend can you define Lyme disease,
When rouged skin's aflame, how tackle ticklish self-reliance?
Is it a scourge of bed bugs or gentle fleas?

My friend, can you define Lyme disease?
Do you need to tame the selfsame villain in this game?
Is it a scourge of bed bugs or gentle fleas?
Do you need to capture one of them, oh please!

Do you need to name the villain in this game?
Moving your bishop to the left or right,
Do you need to capture one of them?
My friend, need we fight the good fight, all night?

Moving your bishop or your knight to the left or right,
To know when you're being eaten alive, my dear.
My friend, need we fight the good fight?
Accursed the room was filled with critters, I swear!

Fishing Tale

When fishing, my grandfather told me: Said,
Throw back the little skipper whence he came
Never hold onto anything you do not need
By eating the little fish the big ones grow tame

Throw back the little skipper whence he came
Don't try to hold onto anything
By eating the little fish, the big ones grow tame
Never hold hostage your soul's awakening

Don't try to hold onto anything
Inspect what you reject but don't get hooked
Never hold to ransom your souls' awakening
Though a line has a time for being spooked

Inspect what you reject but don't get hooked
Imagine you will never confess
Though a line has a time for being spooked
Even a little brother has a time for success

Imagine you will never confess
Never hold onto what you do not need
Even little brother has time for success
When fishing my grandfather told me, Said.

Throw back the little skipper whence he came.

Totem

When a fish leapt from a river, unguessed
Bereft, did anyone receive the message?
Was it a Chilicothy poltergeist
Or something someone prophesied or presaged?

Bereft, did anyone receive the message?
Is there room for little else in our world?
Perhaps something someone prophesied or presaged.
Perhaps a message salvaged from a wave unfurled?

Is there little room for anything else in our world?
What if foxes cavorting in a hollow
Reviewed a message salvaged from a wave uncurled?
Perhaps decoded messages we could not follow?

What if foxes cavorting in a hollow,
Knowing of several riddles of ancient wisdom,
Decoded messages we could not follow
Conceding victories to far distant earthly kingdom?

Knowing of the riddles of ancient wisdom,
Was it a Chilicothy poltergeist,
Conceding a victory to far distant earthly kingdom?
When a fish leapt from a river, what remained unblessed?

Visitation

At night while jumped by several ghosts
As she clocked them in, doors opened and closed.
Whatever way the wind was blowing, she dowsed,
Believing her dreaming more than costly boasts.

As she clocked them in, doors opened and closed.
How could she confess her wisdom's token,
Believing her broken dreaming costly boasts?
All she wanted: unbroken hours of sleep.

How could she define her wisdom's token,
When now and then, she wandered off course?
All she wanted: unbroken hours of sleep
Before the sun had risen in the field of gorse.

When now and then, she wandered off course
Reliving her life through a Tarot reading.
Before the sun had risen on a field of gorse
Roused from her sleep by shades beyond meaning.

Reliving her life by a second reading,
Whatever way the wind was blowing, she dowsed.
Roused from her sleep by shades beyond meaning,
At night, she was jumped by several ghosts

Intermezzo

Her head fell down and banged upon the piano.
That which you thought never occurred.
Her piano teacher hastened from the patio
Why drive the nail deeper than inferred?

That which you thought never occurred.
Neither was she even close to day dreaming.
Why drive the nail deeper than inferred?
What would keep her from half-screaming?

Was she ever close to even day dreaming?
May the scent of lilacs ever increase!
Whatever would keep her from redeeming
The raucous sighs of Canadian geese?

May the scent of lilacs ever increase!
To what do you attribute a lingering dalliance?
The raucous cries of Canadian geese?
Insidious characters of dark disease, held at a distance?

To what do you attribute a lingering fragrance?
Her piano teacher hastened from the patio.
Insidious characters of disease, held at a distance.
Her head fell down and banged upon the piano

Bully-Proof Poem

We found him hanging from a tree
I tried to cut him down myself
However, justice has no mercy
I cried, I yelped, I gave a whelp

I tried to cut him down myself
There was no time to doctor him I cried,
I yelped, I gave a whelp
I caught him by his hanging limbs.

There was no time to doctor him
Can you imagine being his mother?
I cried, I yelped, I gave a whelp.
How could I tell his grandfather?

Can you imagine being his mother?
If saints preserve us, couldn't I save him?
How could I tell his grandfather?
I would that Death forgave him.

If saints preserve us, couldn't I save him?
However, Justice has no mercy.
I would that Death forgave him.
We found him hanging from a tree.

To Lars

What though you squat by oleander
In Kensington in your pajamas,
Whenever you perform at Speaker's Corner,
Spare us your dowsing at Michaelmas, Lars.

In Kensington Park in your pajamas
Though llamas stray while you thumb your yamaha
Spare us your dowsing at Michaelmas, Lars.
As that cat already fat and curled upon that sofa

Though llamas weave while you strum your yamaha
Dare to reinvent that warrior's song
As it is, a cat is already curled upon a sofa
Know your life already owned, but not for long

We knew you'd dare reinvent that song
Why ask God, - you need proof positive?
Know your life already conjoined, but not for long
Whatever you do, be more decisive

Why ask God,- you need proof positive?
Whenever you perform at Speaker's Corner
Whatever you do, be more decisive
Otherwise forlorn, you'll be a goner!

Parallel Lives

Whether I've lived as a cricket in a pond
All I know is I don't belong
The knitted quilt of evensong
In a parallel life beyond the beyond

As a heron standing on one leg
I know I stand stock still or not at all
As a magpie pawning an innocent gig
I know the beginning and end of Myrtle's prattle

Tell me from the beginning of time
Whether the Angel of Bengal existed
Or as a persistent rumor of season's banter
The myth had no reason as insisted.

What though the whispered cry of death
Upon breath's circuitous dance
There is no room for serendipity's chance
When death a hungry spirit out of breath.

Whatever you do, let no harm come to spirit
Knowing full well you live at present, don't forget

Sirens Singing

This what you said, not what you said at all.
The tall ships were not allowed to land
Though welcoming parties somewhat theatrical
Had prepared a big spread, well-planned.

The tall ships were not allowed to land.
Whatever causerie written flew apart
As seamless threads began to whisper contraband
As to the task that divided politics from art

Whatever was said to them that came apart,
And shattered the wits of the most seasoned sailor?
As to the task that divided politics from art,
Inferred from the captain, he might be the jailor.

Shattering the wits of the most seasoned sailor
Imagine a library of the Yiddish book
Could catch universities unaware, or
Could a seasoned crew be escorted off the hook

Eschew a precious library of the Yiddish book?
Despite welcoming parties theatrical
A crew could not be impounded nor off the hook
This what you said, not what you said at all.

Despite all this, the ship embarked to Mexico.

Candlewick Lake

In a narrow aisle of water where she fared
Hopes shattered, she lost the will to dive
How could she remain so unaware
At the last moment with her spirit still alive

Hopes shattered, she lost the will to live
And still the stars could not grant reprieve
Unanchored as her spirit dived, half-decrepit
While sailors swarmed among harmless wave.

And still her friends could not believe
How many wind-surfers jammed the blue lagoon.
While sailors swarmed among harmless sieve-like waves:
Why couldn't she have stayed at home?

How many wind-surfers jammed the blue lagoon
While she reviewed the tactics of blue-nose dolphins
And struggled with past life review, so gruesome
To think she had dabbled in things Machiavellian.

While she struggled with blue nosed dolphins
Come what may, how could she remain so unaware
As she struggled with a past life review, so gruesome
In a narrow aisle of water where she fared

In Candlewick Lake, her soul is still there.

Skunk

Is love the honeyed aphrodisiac
Or like hedgehog stew another matter
For the scientist and the necrophiliac
Instead, baptized upon another platter.

Or like hedgehog strew another matter
My friend, can you redefine your life?
Scarcely you know right speech as banter
Unless a skunk, why downgrade your wife

My friend, can you redefine your life?
Consider the content of that passionate meeting
Unless a skunk, why downgrade your wife
Endured a highly prized blessed beating.

Consider the content of a passionate meeting
Whatever the case, you came in drag
Endured a highly prized blessed beating
In consciousness producing a lag

Whatever the case, you came in drag
For the scientist and the necrophiliac
In consciousness producing a lag
Is love the honeyed aphrodisiac?

Hieroglyph

Despite all this, the ship embarked to Mexico.
Is Death the final aphrodisiac?
Does love inspire a similar awakening?
Though you may endure plenty or lack,
How feast upon the soul's quickening?

Does love inspire a similar awakening?
If you don't know, awake to god, my friend,
Feast upon your soul's synergy.
What though amended truth you bend?

If you don't know, awake to god, my friend.
Why heed the message of the Mayan endgame?
What though the amended truth you bend?
If somewhat myopic, don't walk with a cane.

Why heed the message of the Mayan endgame?
Do you opt for opera- glasses or lorgnettes?
Though myopic lame, don't walk with a cane.
Eschew bagatelles and baguettes.

Do you opt for glasses or vintage lorgnettes?
What though you endure plenty or lack?
Eschew bagatelles and baguettes.
Is Death the final episodic aphrodisiac?

The Art of Swimming

I'm careful about giving out my address,
When I go swimming with relatives.
I'll bury the hatchet on the way I dress
I try to dive deep and stay positive.

Meanwhile when I go swimming with relatives,
While recalling the story, should I digress?
I try to dive deep and stay positive
Do my clothes belong on or off, you guess?

While recalling the story, will I digress?
I try to dive deep and stay positive.
Do my clothes belong on or off, you guess.
I gather,-- too many half-eaten digestives.

Though I try to dive deep and stay positive
Choreographing trance- dances, I hold my breath,
Remaining calm and somewhat meditative
Among the likes of other fast moving fish.

I try to dive deep and remain positive
I'll bury the hatchet over the way I dress
Among the likes of other fast moving fish
I am so careful about giving out my email address.

To Juliette
an Acrobatic Parakeet

What though your parakeet strolls the floor
Foolish though you were handsome though he is
Whatever the outcome don't keep score
Don't worry no one knows your address

Foolish though you were akin to kindness
If you could live your life entranced
Don't worry no one knows your address
Life itself keeps you at a distance

If you could live your life entranced
You might play catch up with pantoum
Life itself keeps you at a distance
Otherwise you might play opposum

You might play catch up with pantoum
Forswearing a buccaneer chappies at noon
Otherwise you might play opposum
And hang upside down before the moon

Forswearing a buccaneer lariat at noon
Whatever the outcome, don't keep score
Hanging upside down before the moon
What though your parakeet strolls the floor

Shaman's Dream

As lilies floated by in undulant stream,
A turquoise bee once ran into a leaf-filled oak tree.
What of the shaman's uninterrupted dream?

Something unexpected in tracking a sample moonbeam
Haunted the sainted Clara to such a hidden degree
While lilies floated by in undulating stream,

While gazing at St. Cuthbert's well, she sensed a frightful scream.
What unimaginable horror did her brain espy?
What of the shaman's uninterrupted dream?

How could she intimate to her husband, Ibrahim
The unspeakable conversation's corresponding melee?
While lifeless lilies floated by in undulating stream.

Now, as she prayed to Quan Yin's thought-stream,
Circumambulating the holy well rather clumsily,
What of the shaman's interrupted dream?

When a lark means business you glean she will redeem
The pithy songs performed before her lord as graceful fealty.
As lilies floated by in undulating stream,
What of the shaman's fitful sleep and unexpected dream?

A Romance of Mortgage Payments

Unused beside his horseman's bed, Knut's Norseman's shallow cloak
No doubt the landlord's crise de coeur revolved around his purse.
Am I still emboldened by the shrill & vengeful cry of sparrow hawk?

Hear how melodious a meadow lark bestirred when Knut awoke
And yet unaccustomed to catching lowing tones,
Knut bespoke a curse
Unused beside his tainted bed, Knut's subtle horseman's cloak

Not like the voice of a spurious sparrow hawk
Who speaks a broken forked tongue language, a wicked ruse
Am I still emboldened by the voice of a sparrow hawk?

A voice that carries sparrows in its clouded wake
We cannot persecute what winds of spirit mistakenly rehearse
Unused beside his bed, Knut's dappled horseman's cloak

While laggard ants crawl close to chalk-ridden sidewalks
Wars are often fought over trifling ways of sinecures
Not yet emboldened by the voice of sparrow hawk

Mankind's only hope is feathered pillow-talk
Unused beside his suburban bed, Knut's Norseman's cloak
Why did Knut blanche at the sight of blood, what's worse
Was he emboldened by the vengeful cry of sparrow hawk
Or something else unrehearsed?

How Eagerly
He Recalled

Demeter's Passing!

Psychomanteum

Look for me, Mr. Odysseus, Mr. Socrates,
At the east gate, – Kanaliki, Ephyra.
Attracting a mirrored ghost surreptitiously,
May I boast the blessing of penance or of grace?

By turning the pages of Mevlevi's book,
At night, I enter the cloister and dance.
To show my love for the faithful, at the shrine,
I have braided tiny rush mats, two at a time.

Why dive so deeply into mirrored flames?
Unafraid, do you imagine soul devouring soul?
If you see a hungry ghost, cover your act,
With juniper, evergreen, and sweetgrass smoke.

Past lives? What elegant hibiscus-filled gardens
In Cordova embrace the width, the length of coffins.
By walking away from oracles, all past indiscretions,
Now may I live this beautiful life, unfettered.

Baptismal Font

Don't gouge out your eyes looking for salvation.
Shadows deepen at St. Winifred's Church Registry.
After souls are entered in the book of life, all is well.
Were I were buried in a pauper's grave,

On the site of a medieval moor,
Drenched in the water of the baptismal font,
Sculpted with chevrons and beak-heads,
Would I have shifted the dust from my feet?

If madness shapes the unseen world of horses,
Having no jeweled harness chosen by priests,
Will sweet grass vapors attend to the lives of those
Who, breaking bread, think they know survival?

If, wind-driven, a field of wheat and barley
Fails a creation story of its own making,
Then, let demons shower curses on my head.
Otherwise, let prayer-soaking go unrehearsed,

Ask: 'What is being drawn to me, exactly?'
Let floor of flesh collapse, overspilling
Close-embered ash of bone and body
Into cave of cloud, sky-lair, palace-heaven.

Death

Unafraid of banal words, Laura remembered,
"Joseph split the face of God and flew.
Halfway out of his body, halfway in,
What keeps you alive? Are ravens crying?"

Where is the dead man's comb? Who cares?
What of the rug pulled out from under him?
Have pockets been turned inside out or not?
Do gold-rimmed spectacles haunt the front mantel?

"Let's shake hands on it, then.
If the common-place is sacred
In this life, why are we whispering to each other?"
She nodded: "You promised,
No matter what we'd stay together."
"Promised what? You mean I do not have to die?"

Who will remember the way Laura read
The evening paper the night before Joseph died?

Parachute-Jumper

Tarnished, the picture of the parachute-jumper.
The eagle-feather fan surrenders its totem.
What ensures grace of White Shell Woman?
Unwinding pine-cones from the hair of Mountain-Dreamers,

Blurred in arcs of arabesque, wave upon wave,
Singing from her holy thighs, her limbs, her arms,
What is this sweet commingling of slanted wings,
Broken upon the belled skirt of innocence?

In furious longing for gold and silver,
Ambushed in rabbit brush, love's memory rests,
Painting iridescent flames in the death-defying
Leaping of Thunder Beings' all-seeing-eyes.

Ceremony

However fleeting this momentary presence,
Let it stand, braiding and unbraiding sacred sashbelts.
In beaded belts of ceremony and thanksgiving,
Love breathing blood and bone at Rosebud Sioux.

Birthing distant almanacs of sound,
Lifting the pattern of a thousand migratory birds,
I've torn open a cloud, a veiled mirage of speech,
A waking dream of oasis. Because I love like this,

I have no sense of consciousness expanding.
Stirring inside a river, when bowing past
The locks, how the wind misinterprets distances.
Who will acknowledge Giuseppe's military funeral?

Return

I let the rabble of goats nibble moss on my roof.
Silence burns the lips of the bearded prophets.
Who has lit a shadow in my tiny room of speech?
A basket of lies holds the pattern. While I'm walking,

Nobody knows the village I am from. No floor.
Before too long, I must sell everything, walk even further.
Silence takes forever to shape the tattoo on my tongue.
I will not ask what the truth of hunger is while you weep.

If befitting to a ghost, you continue weeping, then do.
If not, you understand the secret threads
Your lives cannot unwind.
If silence shapes your tongue, forever muted, so be it.
A thousand thimbles fall like leafy garments to the ground.

II

The one who lives his life through deeds of kindness,
Is unknown. Whatever I purchased from the city,
The money-lender, has retrieved. Place at street-corners,
Why do birds continue to pecking at bread crumbs?

In exile's dignity, we all know we belong to each other.
While memory holds us hostage,
We delight in nothing of the body,
In memory of speech, I revel in the fact
A storm resurrects a heartfelt celebration.

Cave

Don't refer to death as past-life casualty, my friend.
Instead, curve the final breath back into the air.
Faltering for an instant, her voice half-lowered,
Grabbing my arm for emphasis, a widow murmured:

"Maybe being half-demented, my dear,
Or, maybe blind and deaf, or altogether
Lacking, perhaps you are trying
To gain an attentive audience out of fear."

I snipped the roses of her compliments
With chrysanthemum gardening shears.
Disheartened by unspeakable pain,
With an air of complacent wisdom,

Thereafter, I retreated to my cave.

Dying

Unraveling knotted roots of time, I died.
While diving deeper than I dared, I leapt
Into the feathered cloud-windows. Unasked, I found
The restoring of human existence impossible.

I told myself I'd drunk too many cups
Of wine. A thousand alleluias meant
As much to Silenius carousing in painted waterfalls.
While coaxing a knife from Time's hidden sheath,

I asked: "Why doesn't every dervish dance?
While keeping inner and outer knowing soul-drenched,
Overturning a cup of wine, until outpouring love,
How does your body's garment catch its whirling sparks?

"What barber brays when a donkey's ears are snipped?
To keep from dying, is the soul horse-whipped?"

Plant Medicine

Rendering lives as vulnerable as spin-drift,
When winged seeds, flown into codicils and tendrils,
Who will explain a life half-lived, first breath,
Last breath? What signals death's final reckoning?

Existing among stamens, anthers, what is the point
Of a sixteen-branching plant, Goethe's cosmic palm print,
A puzzling physiognomy of medicine harvested?
Luminous and flickering, if love subsides, little by little,

Perhaps multiple lives will be saved by morning.
How endless the wedding of opposites,– a paradox.
Until trade winds die down in Sertung and Panjang,
What makes the body shake with invisible roses?

Whenever covered by a cloud-blanket of ash,
Unasked, your soul will drown completely.

Asphodel

Beneath unlit lamps, you roam inside rooms
Of rain. Ransomed, my soul's suffering,
Unchecked, frail tears fall short of the mark.
Am I beginning a false pilgrimage?

A fevered hunger outlasting measured field,
A thief of time, time's famine falling fast.
Beggared, at the beck and call of games of chance,
Does love outdistance lament
Of half-tilled heaven's acreage?

Measuring distances in nameless labyrinths,
The double-helix of defeat, unwinding love's remembering.
If, when a mountain fire is dowsed, uprooted cypress burn,
Downwind of where you are, a defeated ocean gleams.

Whatever hymns a psalmist learnt to sing,
Heartfelt, do they remain when faith doubts doubt?
Who offers a reprieve for suffering,
Beginning at the beginning?

Clog-Dancing

Believers and non-believers insist on clog dancing.
In the wake of pollen, why do this little dance?
Believers are over-running the logical order
Of the universe. What will it take to stop them?

Before the veiled ones, the soft pony's bridle brags its bells.
Slanted, the tilt of sundial, burning Mother Earth's shadow.
Who impersonates the devil's diadem?
Are you the one with child? Despite the phases

Of the moon, five knights are guests of the harem.
Could the veiled heart be deceived by what it knows?
With her antique broom, an old woman sweeps songs
From beneath wicker wings of snow, newly fallen.

Why tell anyone of the weather of the ancients?
According to the divine will of angels, nothing changes.
If not, how can I trust the act of sitting,
The act of standing? What of nostalgia for the ancestors?

Tongue-tied, those flighty aunts, still dreaming of their past,
While mayflies skirt the wick of water burning.

Mother Earth

Adding to the sadness of existence,
Has the human heart no place within the planet?
Moment to moment, what difference does it make?
Traveling to the stage set of the hogan,

Who am I to will the sundering of threads,
Unraveling ancestor-lineage from Coteau des Prairies?
At times, I feel pulled away, drawn down
Into focal points eclipsed by circumferences.

Knowing full well all is recited perfectly
Within the sculpted song lines of the Dreamtime,
Isn't it true, all is made perfect, blameless,
Watery threads cradled within Manitou's body?

Anchoring blindness, already emerging from darkness,
Will an unlit candle burn its luminous transcendence?
What if a surgeon could suture the harvest
Of winkered waves? What if, uprooted, a mountain

Could forsake the tilted cypress-lantern?
What if cottonwood, if evergreen extinguishing
Its supernatural fire, knelled the tongue
Of an unstruck bell unsinging, yet, still singing?

What of well water sprouting from untilled ground?

Longing

From tureens overspilling holy water,
I turn away. A slight geography of fire,
Her life-breath ebbing, a death-defying leap
Into a momentary landscape singed,

And swarming with meteoric constellations.
Until anchored in weather turned warm,
Perhaps it's best to keep from following the aimless
Track of beggared footsteps' malingering.

Within the unspeakable flame of longing, the love
Of language, as beautiful as the language of silence.
Unless if I see your performance for what it is,–
Language half-glimpsed, half-stripped of mistaken masks,

Shuddering before a shrine of burnt incense-offerings,
Who is the one witnessing a flight of birds?

Threshold

Despite the dark night of the soul, beyond
The flight of bright birds beckoning,
Observing the Nightway Chant within the wedding
Of unspent words, momentarily detained,

Old-time masters continue littering Athenian cages.
Still unopened, unlit husks of dreamers' ripening suns.
If you're the one still weeping, a non-believer
Why subscribe to the misapprehension of unseen things?

Within the canny shape of words
Unharvested and unguessed,
Unsaying the words of all those belonging to me,
What is inferred, that, belonging, I do not belong?
What is the purpose of loving the burden-basket?

Is Malvinia's reason for living based on kindness?
Knowing full well, when feathers touch the cheek,
When wind predicts its own pivotal demise,
When forgiveness is at stake, why hesitate,

Before returning to Mother Earth's precinct?

Kachina

If, as servant to earth's alchemy, truth's half-glimpsed
Body borrowed, pawned, or stolen, don't tell anyone.
Mountain kachinas, hogans, male and female, still persist.
If half-caught in nectared sieves of desert sands,

If, dancing past the deceit of tongue-tied pagans,
While starved of life, a hungry ghost devours
A famine's soured aftermath, then understand
How fearful we are of each other's dreaming ways.

When ocean sparks spindrift to the north, Koskurbeh knows
Human beings come forth to give thanks to Manitou.
Until earth's parallels allow a rooted-vine
To single out its history of sinewed bones,

What kin allowed to buckle underground
In fractured riverbeds, those half-sutured
Souls, wounded by traveling in costly genealogies?
How long must they live unfettered and unguessed?

Labyrinth

If winding-cloths pulled from hidden mounds
Begin springing yucca blossoms in wind-filled,
Banners of tobacco smoke unfurling its wisdom,
How many eyes of maize will sprout endlessly?

While prayer-wheels still decree love's visibility,
Half-way up the mountain, will people,
Detouring from a state of semi-lucid awareness,
Allow no one ceremony to be performed, widdershins?

If a rain dance will not work its magic,
Beyond eclipsing earth's logical shadow,
No one can find a way of pruning earth's particles,
Pertaining to atoms, quarks, molecules of air.

Yet, why should fire-water alone
Inspire a lonely cry reflecting
A beggared hungry soul
Still hungry, yet alive, not whole?

Totem Pole

"Let it be known," my neighbor said, "unless
You say goodbye to your husband, for all you know,
He might visit you beyond the cemetery gates.
Consider the facts, I know your future.

"Marriage vows, though well-meaning, let them go.
Besides," she added, "He never had the nerve
To do the gossipy things you liked to do
Above and beyond the call of duty. Ever find him

"Playing pro-golf tournaments at clambake lunches,
Attending astrological conventions, or literary fêtes?
Had he the courage to amble through
Breeze-ways leading to the guarded entrances

"At Porte de Saint Cloud on the Avenue de Versailles,
Maybe he would have noticed society failed
To defer to muted residues of exclusive forms.
Off duty, these cultural norms often deemed appropriate

"Causing epiphanies for those erecting totem
Poles in front of distant convent walls."

Black Hills

Black Hills Gold. Small match box holding ashes.
For my late husband, degrees of love made no difference.
From the beginning, he had me fully pegged,
Inferred from unmet dreams,– the what-might-have-been.

As unseen counterpoint to night blindness,–
Bluebirds, lilies, pruning shears,
Shaker chairs, window boxes, gladiolas,
As well as the dug-out log canoe, so Indian to us.
Wherever the stammering river music took us, I followed.

Today, I flow, I go with it, I grow with the-ghost-of-love,
Sister, carrier of the two-fisted pail, mother,
Handkerchief-festooned aunties, elders, I know you must
Enjoy walking in a momentary fire

Of tulips, crocus-blooms, begonias, semantic idioms.
In death's aftermath unheard of in the Yap District,
Until the Milky Way yields up its wine,
Dive more deeply into the planetary mind.

Gate House

I told her, "I will not settle in that house.
Most people have to learn to sit for years
Before purifying their bodies." "There is no cure
For grief," she said. "There is no cure for you."

The you-or-the-not-you in my life,– I note the way,
Lingering in doorways, I miss a door jamb or two.
The small ways I have of living naturally,
Have suddenly been pulled out from under.

Staying in the house when I should have left,
Laughing, when you spoke, "No doubt you'll learn
To sink or swim." Later while standing motionless
In partita's ensemble of oboe-players,

You'll dance a dizzy waltz filled with regret.

Soothsayer's Dream

Trying to predict who wins at poker, I wonder
Will God untangle synaptic branches of the brain?
Knowing you'd still question how angels guide mankind.
If gnat-catchers exorcise ghosts of ant-larvae,

What stock of locusts would spring past slats of time
Mapped by *Disquistiones Arithmetica*?
When ground swells with sculpted cenotaph,
Who blames who when lion-ants dip into fire-filled pits?

The soothsayer promised I would have a daughter, Nadia.
We would live in Northern New Mexico forever.
And then we dreamt we climbed those peaks in Yosemite.
Where we concluded most trees grew antlers of antiquity.

When gleaning an understanding of what we're not,
Two distinct Creators must have been at work.

Self-Portrait

When bird-shaped clouds nourish an ill-defined cocoon,
Does Laura describe herself as sparrow or as wren?
If first breath, last breath yearns for blessing then,
Alphabets may vex grammar's impermanence.

When light is driven towards light, history seeks reply.
Standing before a mirror, Laura hears God's voice.
Terra firma. Feeling unfit to move ahead,
What light will lead her towards Daemon's labyrinth?

Binding her to what is akin to her soul's language,
First Woman appears with White Buffalo. In keeping
With what is sacred, she bows before a shrine
From which deer have fled, then looks the other way.

While escaping a soothsayer's destiny she awaits,
She sits, she opens a scripted book of life.
Now a hidden sage becomes familiar,
More mysterious, she sees him moving away from her.

Mirror

As weaver of dream-harems, often visions redefine her.
Within a dowry of winding roads. Sometimes, she grows
As lazy as a gardener tending to vertiginous gardens.
After checking water in a briar-filled pail,

She waits. Attendant upon the seventh gate,
What causes her to stagger towards a finite thing?
A rose, perhaps filled with what is infinite?
Fragrance that stops regret as easily as sleep?

In a yellowed forest of a thousand birds,
A leafless branching form of formless forms,
Songs moored in the dreamtime invoke echolalia.
Relying on a sashbelt, she senses danger:

Harvested from a coat-of-many-colors,
Her body drenched in sorrowful joy,
She almost wakes before she dreams of death.

Why Doesn't the Body

PART
III

Remember How to Dance?

Enlightenment

Using inked scrolls, I recall learning how to read.
Although the younger generation found the truth,
I've been looking up old friends' addresses everywhere,
In codicil-filled alphabets, in scripted documents, I've found

Ways of discerning the genuine,
Ways of extracting the counterfeit.
Dowsing for diseases, I avoided schools beggaring trust.
Scattering calendulas and roses on leaf-strewn estates,
Clearly, I avoided breaking jaywalking rules.

Now I defer to the left-handed pruning shears
Of gardeners on vacation doing the dog-paddle.
Having learnt moves at backgammon and at chess,
After reading handbooks for the lame,

After signing for the deaf, dumb, and blind,
I perused indices guiding those preferring
Vacation spots including seaside places
At Galway, Blackpool, Liverpool, or Cardiff.

Awakening

Grandmother Bird refuses to spread out her wings,
What for? Doesn't she know the world sings
Of birds drawn down from every cloud-gable
By auctioneer's gavels?
Clearly spiritual fires need quenching.

While feathered talons chime with wind-branches,
She asks, when do you know you need to travel?
Without knowing it,
You've tangled the hair of alder blooms.
Arching over roof, or over verandah's stairway,

What of the body's intelligence? Do you perceive
A second story, roof, floor, and ceiling walls
In continuous patterned sequences all-encompassing?
What deepens a nexus of elemental cells still forming?

If love's spark flickers and goes out, if later,
In unrelenting darkness, a god-demon appears,
Retracting laws of gravity, before birthing.
Logos, what then, what next? To allay our fears,

We reinvent the history of Lao-Tse, Leh-Tsu.

Birds

Undreamt of now, the riches of a thousand birds.
Perhaps, among these most silent branches,
Mystic ones are already bending leaves in spring.
About that dying ghost, it may be Winter's loss.

Whoever is embarrassed at grieving Autumn's death,
What brings the whittled bone-wings of bird's awakening?
In Winter, in Summer solstice, does pick and shovel work
Befit the cost of death? At what cost, life, death's refrain?

Motionless, I lie on my back. The sky appears
The same and yet, brimming with burrs, gnats spar.
Leading to the merchant's house, the road map
Eclipses my knowing where it led. Before slipping

Into another's voice, this year I despaired
Of knowing the rooms that distanced us,
From one another. Who grapples with a bear,
May muzzle a stray dog to make amends.

Knowing how many friends bear witness to dying,
My pony lifts her head. Does she hear something?
Nothing but silence! Stars burning overhead,
What makes gods banter back and forth?

We're here or maybe not. Inside villages,
Invisible seeds germinate in slow motion.
Question: What force resides inside a stone?
You might as well sing tomorrow to a thorn-tree
Than to a rose bush, when butterflies begin to swarm
Over the field of cypress trees
Heading to Mother Earth's fountain.

Heart

When we dislike a person, the mouth pulls down.
Within a gaze that's steady and unbroken,
Grief feeds on shame's despair until regret's
Unbidden wings fly from leaf-strewn thickets.

Before the eyes of the Beloved, elusive blossoms
Bloom unveiling saffron-colored robes.
If you agree that spring revives the body,
I'll call my neighbor and declare the blind

Can see. If a heart collapses in an instant,
Uprooting sanctuary of selfsame rooted tree,
With the interstitial passing of each cell,
Upon hearing how it went, who will lament

The passing of each solitary rose,
Each widowed weed outdistancing this life?

Invocation

Mo-Ti, Chung-Tse and other philosophers
Prefacing Elijah, Jeremiah, Heraclitus,
Thucydides, Parmenides. When a sage refuses to speak,
How many demons are extracted from the fire?

Vanishing into a non-existent darkness.
As truth unwinds a labyrinth of dreams,
How distant then a sylvan parable,
Forget-me-knots blooming at Lake Champlain.

Observe the golden rays refracting sapphire mirrors,
Retracting gleaming amethyst-driven leaves.
Isn't this the place where Daphne appears
Among sacred statues at St. Columbus Monastery?

Rooted in place, only a stone's throw's away
Before imagined proximities of grace,
Open the eastern gate!

Wampum

If believers and non-believer alike, insist
On clog-dancing in the wake of fancy dancing
Contests, what feathered deities will slay us in spirit?
Why confound the drowning logic of the sleep-walker?

This little step-dancing forum is full of inconsistencies.
Overturning Tibetan brass begging bowls,
Rose-petals dream back the bones into the blessed body,
A theatrical piece held over by popular demand.

Is this another life or is the present one more costly?
Owning every bird song, branching inwardly,
Over-spilling water renders better cause
For incantatory divination practice.

Why argue with a haunted dervish palace?
Roses bloom the same way, whatever Truth's garden.
Suffering has its place within the darkness and the light.
Fading into forgotten darkness, soon, Mr. Whipperwill,

Will learn to untie the dark shoelaces of the moon,
The hidden wedding feast. What of the unbidden
Guests of the sheik, so drunk, that, slamming into walls,
They cannot be dispassionate about anything.

Soon, you won't understand the perfume of my words.
How is it with you, in any shape or form,
I do not hear you sparring:
Needesh granny ah, mineivis Iuba I toree?

Before the veiled wings of sleep,
A pony's bridle brags its bells.
Why dream of dying, especially
When you're the one just born?

Aleuts

Lake Chautauqua is the place the sages
Will accompany her, for better or for worse.
Or to some-other-god-forsaken-place.
Fiercely supernatural, she knows Mt. Kailash.

As many years as she's been walking Mother Earth,
She's always seen lugging garden furniture.
At daybreak, she's up to say goodbye to many
Waiting by the fence. I see Brother Cougar,

He, too, may want to catch a Nightway chant.
As for myself, selling otter-pelts, I'm heading north.
I'll live at a north fork of a river where wind
Brings shape-shifting to a close, where stars elope

And the tree you stand next to begins to dance alone.

Dowry

Don't hammer this corpse thing into the ground. Perhaps,
Someday you will be introduced to someone new.
Laura mediated on the very question:
You'd promised who would meet me after dark?

He's only been dead in the grave a year, and still
You took it upon yourself to dishonor me until
I asked you, what you take me for, a fool?
The dead never die this way in Biloxi, Mississippi.

Hotel room in Berea. Didn't his daughter
Alarm you somewhat, telling you the story:
Your bride is a bear from Kentucky, watch her closely.
A person with crazy wisdom,
Could be dragged down by her.

Later, withdrawing into your body's ghost,
Changing your mind, you'll want her back to dance
With you at a Country-and-Western Jamboree,
A get-together that will end all speculation.

Loss

The funeral arranged itself in Cripple Creek.
Teeming with ashes, a Tang dynasty vase is still.
I note you've put up an altar next to his photo.
Who says we must take a second look at life?

Brakes scream. The beloved priest speaks of death.
Time makes an old believer more divine.
What would the relatives be wanting with his coat?
Inform me as to the way in which you would

Align this beggared trading post of minutes,
If never sold at all, consider the great love
A star-quilt holds. With jingle-dance's awakening,
Beaded moccasins draw the family thread.

Grove's Dictionary of Music contains thirteen volumes
Rerouting innkeepers' dreamtime as old as ancient maps.

Shaman Wife

"Bring in the wood so we can start the fire," the brother says.
From the frozen lip of the skillet, the old fish spits.
Beside the bow and arrow we use for squirrels,
The fish hook used for sealskin-sewing on the wall.

"You know they're going to take you back into the fold,"
Her brother sighs. "Now," the old woman cries,
"Husband, do you think about me sometimes?"
Mostly, she's been calling out to relatives

Through mist-filled ethers in her sleep. "All night,
You've heard her singing to the bears." Her brother
Shrugs his shoulders, embarrassed by his sister
Seeing a ghost reflected on the lake. "Who knows

"About her husband, she won't leave off keening.
Leave-taking makes all the difference to our elders."
"I don't think that much about him," the old hag lies.
Her whispered voice sounds like a plover's windpipe

Or that of an otter, seal pup, or speckled quail.
In a way to deflect a stranger, her brother offers,
"People say she's on her second husband now.
I sure can tell you this, I don't know how I know."

Afterlife

To say nothing of death, in any case, Dr. Fever
Took her with him to the end the road, the afterlife.
Downwind of where he was in the hereafter,
As he led her, she sighed, surrendered, and slid,

Ether-bound, into Isiphan's dark caves.
Those caves formerly used to sequester the dead.
To begin dancing over the bridge of death,
To begin piercing the dark lair of heavy-lidded light,

A traveler need not be deceived by irreverence.
Let souls cross over tiny rivulets without regret.
If one confesses to swallows and to birds,
That snow whitens the hair, then peach blooms felled

From gossamer branches zig-zagging everywhere,
Drawing down a vast snow-filled calligraphy of air.
Then, when the soul decides to retreat above
Into a sacred star-filled canopy of sound,

No one should be surprised when transcendent
Spirit like a wind-horse walks on feathered roofs.
Do not grieve over what has already happened,
With light snuffed out, ember's softened gleaming.

Guest-House

I said that I would settle here in that house.
Most people sit in practice for years
Before bones are purified. At what cost,
For discernment or detachment's boast,

As, one by one, guests withdraw to the tavern,
Not really a greenhouse? I'd be willing to bet
What people make of death, more than what
They make of life. Who cares if you will a brain

To science? Supposing logic's odds are stacked
For or against? Tarot cards are ordinary pictures
For soul's decoded shadows brought to light.
While goat herds melt in thorn-filled deserts,

In a maggot-infested sea where reflections die
In the refracted light of mirrors disguised as demons,
What drives you to drink, as night thicken its palsied ghosts,
Softening those harsh voices of cricket-filled rain?

Transcendence

Don't think that Columbus discovered America.
We've been over and over this terrain before.
Since China birthed the first explorers we might
As well bequeath our bones to whatever shore,

Without recalling region of birth and heritage.
How will this lineage look to the gentry, good enough?
Pegging stones at herons, kestrels, ospreys,
Walking away as if nothing had ever happened.

Orphaned, how can one abandon country?
Do graves sprout bright parishes of leaves?
You cannot blame the outer robe for grieving ghosts.
Colder, oddly inward. Old passport stamps.

My husband sings and flees to the Ivory Coast.
It's not for my husband that I grieve, but a siege
Of the mind as found in eagle-rug patterns,
Those holding the crania of twenty-four Turkish sailors.

Wandering off course, supposing a pilgrim detoured,
Criss-crossing ley lines within a New York street map?
What is the source of a transient nostalgia,
But a romance of awakening in a time-machine.

Havelinas

Dreaming of madness, when havelinas bark,
While entering star-filled fakirs' caves,
As kennel-keepers yield their places, wild dogs
Run free. What better bargain could be struck

Than wordless music flying through the spine
Where music meshes with body and spirit's flesh.
As you open the book of life you witness
Small birds suddenly falling silent on the wing.

Releasing the spirit-clothing from the muse,
The midwife knows how to cut the rose.
Hidden in her perfumed lair,
For years, havelina repeats a never-ending talk story.

As heart dividing heart drowns in wren-filled ocean,
Your soul breaks open, love-riven.
That's when we find we are all travelers on the road,
Grasping for heaven's blessing and grace.

Hemlock

Coyote is no sleight-of-hand tarot-pack shyster.
Well-versed in the art of dress rehearsal,
How can he carry on affairs with marathon-runners
Already out of stamina and muscle?

Who listens to the ebb and flow of bird songs,
Half-remembered the days of monotonous frog-voices,
Signaling unrelenting rain, drumming overhead?
As sound effects for displaced persons multiply,

Prisoners known to have lived other lives,
Exit, unguessed in time's fated equation.
If, witnessing an hour-glass overspilling sand,
The length of your days, shortened, lengthened, pruned,

Like seamless broadcloth cut away, as contraband.
In a split second, breath may surrender breath,
Displacing unearned income credits pawned.
Until you find yourself listed in a book of names,

Your baptism unexpected, misshapened, and prolonged.
Though once you thought a year had scarcely flown.

Mercy

As blind seer, a beloved priest speaks of death.
At times, this makes an old believer seem divine.
What would travelers have wanted with these bones?
Who informed you needed more time within

A beggared trading post of minutes, maybe hours?
If bartered, bought, and sold, what if the star quilt
Still held the pox, who could punish god
For failing to annex human misery?

Whether you've pegged stones at great blue herons,
Don't ponder the meaning of the holocaust.
Later, would you walk away as if nothing had happened
To Nature's heart? Instead, you may suffer staggering

From a lake you never honored. How can you blame
An outer robe for growing inwardly cold?
Make no mistake about it, lady, didn't you say
Your husband's brother, a convicted killer of promises?

While leaves continue sprouting parables of truth,
Doesn't the miraculous border on madness somehow?

You Haven't a Clue as

PART IV

to How to Play House!

Library

Each time I take the book back to the library,
I note a dozen pages are torn out.
Graffiti names scrawled carelessly throughout.
Perusing back-jacket covers, I wonder, who's the culprit?

Is this the handiwork of Jack or Jill,
Steeplejacks, stevedores, janitresses, or what?
Perhaps underwriters of insurance policies
Have censored or burned all antique pages

Containing recipes for "Milk of Acorn" stew.
Alchemy. Alone in shade-house, I watch the way
Jittery paraffin lamps hiss and go out.
Awakening, I drown in the fire of Arcturus.

Reflecting on the mysteries of caliphates,
I am contemplating the latest wedding album.
Finding five turbaned men sleeping in Isiphan's cave,
I have chosen not to disown any of them.

Traveling past interwoven bloodlines, as horses
Yoked together, bartered, bought, or sold,
Are we still seers refusing a blessing
Well-schooled in the art of vanishing?

Household

Where are you, man of the house? I keep asking
In a dream that will never be done. Over and over,
I remember slamming screen doors in your face.
Have you ever thought of returning from Chicago?

In the company of men, women, and children, I dream
Of a mountainous region swarming with centipedes.
Slanted like shadows, red prairie hens were on the run.
I never had anything to say about love's return.

Where are you, man of the house? I keep asking
In a recurring dream never fully completed,
In my heart of hearts, I wonder whether the door is locked?
Knowing full well the kitchen door left open.

You know me well enough, man of the house,
I say. I see those dream figures unraveling,
Shadows moving on a mountain meadow,
Those red prairie hens on the run.

Castanet-Player

Once, I heard a gypsy tell a castanet-player,
'Angel Gonzales, tonight I'll sing until
I'm hoarse. Let no one insult us,
Not even the wide-eyed tourists from Grenada.'

When preaching future lives in Malaga bordellos,
If jackdaws sing happily ever after, Amen!
Who knows how many chariots will burn?
Played for pennies raining down on tavern floors,

Why do mandolin-players sing of betrayal?
Until flamenco soul-wings glowed like frozen statues,
Treblinka gypsies dance in furnace-ovens.

Siberian Autumn

Undreamt, the riches of a thousand birds,
Who will listen to my secrets one
That I am old and fear the sleeping embers
Of the heart? The ghost that grieves in spring

Is the ghost that weeps in turn for autumn.
Fear sings of a map of famine that sleeping grieves,
A tongueless silence, reckoning up accounts.
Where butterflies swarm over waterfalls, obelisks

Castle walls, pagoda surrender saints
Before painted iconography
An orchard vision is but a surface light
Embroidered in prayer's elusive fire whose inner

And outer flame belies incandescent form.
Therefore, wash the feet of the Siberian groom,
Then drink the transparent water of heirloom.

The Ur-pflanze

I've packed up everything...I've sold my straw pallet.
I've sold my cows, my goats, my sheep. I've been looking
For something along the river banks.
To reveal the nameless plant
Would be a sacrilege of what is ordinary.

I have buried an antique fan at the foot of the mountain,
A long way away from where I live, the dead
Pass quickly when they go, a long time ago,
I preferred to linger in the shadows at home
And read almanacs, calendars and pamphlets

Containing the details of goddess,
The origin of migratory planets
The ways the body can be retrieved
From the underworld of desire
Defining a particular flower belonging to Erishkigal.
At home, but now, I want to travel.

Cassis blossoms define my longing for what is impossible
For nothing that is reasonable,
My grandmother, the dowager,
You know the lady from the old country,
The weaver of icons,
She's the one that creates all the trouble.

Soul Retrieval

I

I let the rabble of goats nibble moss on my roof.
Silence burns the lips of the bearded prophets.
Who has lit a shadow in my tiny room of speech?
A basket of lies holds the pattern, but where I'm walking

Nobody knows the village I am from.
There is no floor.
Before it's too late, I sell everything,
And walk to the next village.
Silence takes forever to shape and tattoo on my tongue.
I will not ask what the truth of hunger is while you weep.

If it is befitting to a ghost that you should weep, than do.
If not, then understand the secret place
Your life cannot unbend.
If silence shapes your tongue forever mute, so be it.
A thousand thimbles fall like my leafy garment.

II

He who lives out his misery in kindness..
Now that is something not to be believed.
Whatever I purchased from the city
The money lender has retrieved. All his birds are placed
At a corner of the village where they peck at crumbs.

And ask for nothing of deliverance.
This is the dignity of exile, we all belong to each other.
We hole hostage nothing of the body, only memory,
The memory of speech.
I delight in the fact a storm resurrects

The body and slides down
The hair of the mountain who sings.
Is nothing yet to be believed?
The Milky Way contains the hive full of souls
The unborn bees that have not learned to dance on flowers

Parable

What is the song of death?
What is the song of breath?
What is the song for weaving?
What is the song for living?

What is the song of a birthing ceremony?
Will we leave for the country tomorrow?
What hand trembling remembers its awkward quests,
Its raven night visitors,
Who are they exactly?
Those people who come in droves?

How does the river comb the invisible hair of otters
Each morning, why do I drown at dawn?
How is it night visions lead naturally
To the green keening cry of plant medicine?
Breathing naturally, how do you walk into an open field,

Into a sky leading into a crescendo of flowers?
For those who remember,
I want to know who is responsible?
Who takes the time to spread out the table,
The altar cloth for the invisible?
For the great wedding feasts of the invisible
Are somehow made visible.

What if, still singing, every star broke open, like a parable
Told within the living life span of each
Four-foot and two-foot creature?
What if every star broke open in the perfume of the dawn,
Breathing light of its narrow orchards into cells,

Cells still singing with its birds,
Still singing, still crying, still weeping,
Between twin ponderosa pine needles,
What is exchanged?
A four-handed miracle
Is not enough to keep widows away.

Success

I keep chocking when I get to the good part of my life.
I'm heavily influenced by the sound
Of the kettle drum and the tenor when it gets this good
And the vibrato, the raised alarm of total awareness.
Later, as it eases out of that crescendo, I want to
Bail out gracefully, of course, but bail out, for sure.
Return the compliment by running out of gas right there
On the prairie where the orchestra once was (although
They moved out of town at least seven years ago).

Finally, I want to slap a mosquito, make some outward
Gesture about the inner self, let it go splat right
There in the dust and lay down and spell out
The particular perpendiculars about my coffin.
At least I will have the details down,
Know exactly what to expect after success like that,
Watch the footprints surround themselves, pretend
They're echoes after the real thing has cleared off
And drowned after success
Like that, after success has drowned
Me.

Water

Without the water of the body, we could not
Live at all, not predicate the weather of the soul.
The water you want may drown you in clairvoyance,
Refusing to make you full of wisdom, dutiful, cheerful.

Among dreadful piles of bones, plenty of ghosts
Will be introduced to you as son-in-law, mother-in-law,
Yet anyone of them you envision sitting,
Standing, walking may not revisit you.

When one day Blue Jay returns from fishing,
Half expecting him to put out several
Prairie fires in the land of the living, his aunt
Asks him to obey her. Still she does not.

Instead, he makes misleading statements about
The nature of war. In the process of mistaking
A salmon-colored painting for a metaphor,
He deserves all the while a stone canoe.

Hidden Arabesques

That's what he said she did all her life
In hidden arabesques that neither held
Nor hid any moral sense of outrage
About his sense of life that did and did not matter,
What else could he do but cry for Enikdu
His former wife now lay dead
In the front parlor? The mantel leaning
Into a frozen fire. Embers leaping. Desire:

The Romance of Enikdu

What little left to do but cry
In the front parlor, but cry,
Do little else but that.
As it is, love is not enough.
At the memory of the orishas?
Unseen assailants he called ghosts.
But what were ghosts? Gusts of wind?
Contracts rescinded with flesh?

Apologies

What if I told you I never loved you?
Dear Sir, I beg to differ, I just apologize
I never loved you. Your cold knuckles
Impersonated nothing I want to remember.
My mother used to tell me: when you get older
Mark my words: you will be found out under a bridge.
That's why you'll never live long enough
To make a stone soup out of your bones.

Reverie

More than enough to tell you
No more than this reverie in silence:
Had she lived but a little while longer,
What stories I might have told her.
While she was still in the body, I confess
I never scolded her.

The Ivy on the Wall

I let thoughts creep
Up on me as the invisible ivy continues
Creeping up on the garden wall
Outside the window in the front parlor.
He'd never had that much to do
Who had she been? A wife? A friend?
A neighbor's wife? Not much more than that?
Can I break the news to her now?

Up Close and Personal

I never cared for her overmuch.
I never cared for you overmuch.
Is that what I would tell her?
For the art of love-making to touch
Don't go there. Don't go. Don't go there.
To love overmuch.
Was picture framing an improbable act
A surreal excuse for not dancing in outer space?
Or is the cosmos only an unjust
Cause celebre for using metaphor?

Understudy

Cold as a revolver, her cheek.
As the giver of life, who was the understudy?
For the undertaker's position?
Shall we have aperitifs
Are they not now in order?

The Unravelling of Silence

Beginning here a momentary unraveling of silence
As if love, silver haired and demure
A sinecure and subservient to dreams of dalliance
As with another man's paramour.
Such dreams that can outdistance and slacken
The length of the dreams of little men.
Small of stature magician of lust,
His thirst for life now drenched in blood.
A fevered murmuring, is that what he says he heard?

Stone Cold Heart

His heart knew nothing of feeling.
He says he listens for memories from a far off room.
A room filled with heaped up piles of discarded rosaries.
Wasn't it her mahogany dresser drawer the one left half- open?
Oh yes, he'd covered her body with kisses.
He did what was expected of one that was bereft.
He was very good at that sort of thing.
 A leftover hangover peeling off from a gust of wind,
Wallpaper fading with perfumed dahlias
Littered with swatches of baby's breath.
Until fear has no father and no mother

Global Warming

This week alone, did you know
They are in the process of killing of mute swans?
If death a lament of a most hotly contested divorce,
In a hastily murmured aside and as a retreat from farewell,
Is that suffix or prefix appropriate
As for a surreal cremation or burial?
At the bottom of the stairwell, the bearded captain waits

The Courage to Fear

What could he tell himself he really feared
Unheralded messages from the grave?
Time that knows how to forgive
The unforgivable whatever that is.
Now the discarded jargon of innocent pilgrims
Once pushed away in youth
Clamoring for recognition in old age.
Isn't innocence part of the wisdom
The distance of that great divide,
Drowning the flesh of two people
No longer able to hide from one another,
Both swimmers awash in the tide
Of first breath, last breath, the onset
Of the catch in the chest, the hasp
Retired upon the latch of the fence.
Once reviled, a black and white television is left on.

Captain Fever

Dr. Fever. Dr. Death.
A Doctor Kevorkian fated from the first
And too late.
Waited for days for her to return.
The sickening stench of her perfume
Lingering in every room.
Life no longer sweet.

Chasm

She crossed over, that's all I know
That's what he told a neighbor. She crossed over.
The neighbor crosses herself. Normally, Mrs Black
Lives in the outback on a houseboat
Situated somewhat closer to the Pensacola coast.
Occasionally she comes to visit her sister
Who lives in the upstairs flat.
While his wife gained dominion over her body:
That's precisely what he told Mrs Black
Such as she was, his wife used to do.
And I mean continuously.
And what was that? Mrs Black used to also ask.
Outlived her commitment to the privilege
Of her sex and gender.

The Pianist

With his anger no longer appearing
So appealingly counterfeit or transparent,
Apparently he'd gone and hired a pianist for the funeral.
On summer nights he listened for her.
He said he never missed the light of shooting stars before.
This occurred at a time when crickets
Were in the habit
Of dancing outside in tall grass
At a time when singing as prisoners
Inside bamboo cages
The moon did what it could to dissuade him
From taking his own life.

About author
Elizabeth Martina Bishop Ph.D

Elizabeth Martina Bishop writes prose poems, prose, essays and short stories and is currently undergoing the acquisition of a second doctorate in women and spirituality at CIIS/ San Francisco. She also blogs for Patheos.com, a religion and spirituality site.

Previous to that, she acquired her third MFA at CIIS under the tutelage of Carolyn Cooke. She also appeared in the San Francisco Litquake in 2012.

Bishop has her books on sale at Amazon.com and sells direct at various fairs around the country.

Interested in developing poems for the stage and developing her skills as a playwright, she has produced seveal verse plays and monologues.

Please visit her website at www.ElizabethMartinaBishop.com to view a recent selection of her work as well as the "Poem a Day" selection. In addition, she has published more than 50 collections of poetry.

Books by Elizabeth Martina Bishop

Elizabeth has published close to 50 poetry collections.
All books available through Amazon.com.
Here is a small selection of her work.

The Goddess Lives
at the Columbus Caffe

These photos and poetry gathered here reflect the
creative bridge in communication alternating
between meditative image and the power of words.

The life of the bohemian poet is revealed, the
aesthetics of image is reproduced for your enjoyment
in order to
jump start the reader's imagination.

ISBN-13: 978-1511473569
ISBN-10: 1511473568 • $11.95

Selected Poems

The poems in this collection represent a distillation of Bishop's works and showcase her sense of humor, as well as her whimsical approach to the art of writing poetry. While the parameters of her wide ranging poetic style are influenced by 'sound poetry' and her affection for performance art, she stands in favor of the idea that poetry may return us to a spiritual place that invokes a ravishing journey of inner awareness, peace, and soulful contemplation.

ISBN-13: 978-1507527849
ISBN-10: 1507527845 • $25.25

Words Not Yet Spoken

These photos and poetry gathered here reflect the creative bridge in communication alternating between meditative image and the power of words.

The life of the bohemian poet is revealed, the aesthetics of image is reproduced for your enjoyment in order to jump start the reader's imagination.

ISBN-13: 978-1505863673
ISBN-10: 1505863678 • $9.95

Tunnel Vision

Tunnel Vision expresses a kind of open and reverent supplication before Mother Earth's wintery and windswept altars. Elizabeth Martina Bishop certainly welcomes the chance to spread out her wings as we humans must try to endure climate change.

What if poets did not possess umbrellas and overcoats? So many people succumb to the numbing cold of winter; yet in extremes of temperature, many find a kind of a peaceful way of life without feeling lost.

Knowing each snowflake is an entirely different jewel may be the start of a new poem.

ISBN-13: 978-1505460551
ISBN-10: 1505460557 • $10.99

Printed in Great Britain
by Amazon

42601284R00067